girls&

To Addison and Juliette,

Don't let perfection stand in your way,
or competition shrink your worth, and
always *always* help the girls around you
believe they deserve more, too.

**TO THE REMARKABLE WOMEN
I'VE MET THROUGH LIFE, YOUTH
ORGANIZATIONS AND MY WORK,**

It's your stories, your strength, and your struggles
that inspire me to be brave, go deeper,
and introduce this work earlier in a woman's
journey in order to build a world that
is deserving of us and our girls.

A WORKBOOK

girls & 

THE ULTIMATE GUIDE FOR EMPOWERING A GIRL IN YOUR LIFE

JOAN KUHL

Table of Contents

Dear Reader,

Have you ever worried that a girl you care about doesn't fully accept all the wonderful things you see in her?

This question is the stimulus for *Girls &*, a workbook that equips grownups with the tools, knowledge, and resources to empower their girls, and teach them strategies to strengthen their self-worth. Ultimately, we hope to grow girls' confidence, determination, and ambition, and strengthen their belief that they deserve to achieve their potential. I'm happy to report that, with the support of trusted grown-ups and respectful friends around them, it's possible. Whether you have picked up this workbook because you want to empower your daughter, niece, or younger sister, or whether you are a mentor for young girls, I am grateful to you for showing up. This workbook was designed for grown ups to use *alongside* the girl they care about. By reflecting on things together, this book works on two levels. First, it covers multi-faceted, dynamic topics that are crucial to her development; second, it sends a message to your girl: *she can count on you.* By picking up this book, and taking the time to explore together, you are showing her that you are her fiercest advocate.

Before I dive into how to use this workbook, I want to share why this means so much to me.

I'm a mom of two daughters, a big sister, and I have a long history of involvement in organizations that serve girls (*Girls Inc. of NYC, Girl Scouts, Girls Hope, Step Up for Women, US Soccer SheBelieves, Girls On The Run, Girls Leadership,* and *LiveGirl*). I've served as a board member, content designer, coach, and volunteer because I believe in the power of mentorship, and that investing in a girl's self-confidence can accelerate her leadership skills and impact in the world. After 14 years of working at global corporations, I launched my business in 2013, with

the mission to advance and retain women in the workplace, and to build inclusive cultures where women of all ages and stages can thrive. Leveraging my expertise in Gender and Generation Dynamics, I conduct global research studies, advise corporations and business schools, and facilitate training and consulting engagements in five time zones. Early in my entrepreneurial journey, I was the career expert for Barnes & Noble College – leading research and running workshops for their network of 750+ schools of five million plus students. The time I spent researching and exploring our youngest generation's motivators deeply informed my vision for building inclusive, equitable workplaces.

In the earliest years of my life, I watched my mother take risks to embrace her ambition, and this instilled in me a belief that girls and women have the right to pursue their potential. For almost the first decade of my life, she raised me as a single mother, and did her best with the knowledge and resources she could access. But things got tough, especially when her confidence was tested working in a male-dominated field. Back then, there was nothing like what is available today for grownups who want to empower their girls. While things have improved, there is room for growth, and I am convinced that my strong voice and perspective can make a difference.

So, where do we start? I believe strongly in the impact of programming, education and tools intentionally designed to empower girls and strengthen their self-worth. We must openly and proactively teach them how to defy stereotypes and overcome biased barriers that activate self-doubt. We must strive to disrupt the pervasive negative, unhealthy messaging that permeates media and culture.

I've spent thousands of hours online and in-person, during my leadership workshops and coaching sessions exploring women's struggles and breakthroughs in 30+ countries. I spend a significant amount of time researching tested methods, new strategies, and building resources that enable me to offer concrete solutions. This is triggering work, and hearing women struggle across so many spectrums of life is hard. Which is why I am determined to make a difference _earlier_ in a woman's life. I specifically designed this workbook to target girls aged 6-12. Why? Around the age of eight, girls' confidence takes its first noticeably-steep dive. Research shows that not only does their confidence plummet by 30% through

age 14, but anxiety rates have skyrocketed over the past ten years. These alarming statistics impact so many aspects of girls' and women's lives, from decision-making to relationships. *Girls &* aims to disrupt this cycle earlier – before the confidence rollercoaster begins – in order to radically alter its track, and create a smoother ride for girls.

But, of course, there is another huge source of inspiration for *Girls &*...**my own girls**. As the mother of two daughters (Juliette, 6, and Addison, 10), I am constantly juggling my pursuit to better understand their challenges, and proactively use this knowledge to support them and keep them safe. Sometimes I was able to find resources that gave me answers and ideas; other times I was left short and had to improvise. While there will never be a perfect playbook, I truly believe that the more we share and experiment, the more we create opportunities that will provide a positive difference.

While writing this book, I was determined to follow my own advice, and carve out space to reflect with Addison and Juliette. Throughout the guide, I share my bumps in the road, as well as the breakthroughs that have taught me key lessons, such as how we can deeply connect, be present with, and support our girls in mindful moments. But, as you'll see, it's been far from an easy ride! There were moments when my effort to jumpstart a conversation with my girls was awkward and not met with the enthusiasm I had hoped for. But that's ok. What counters these moments are the conversations that worked; those that stretched us, and offered space to develop a meaningful connection. Through all my professional and personal experiences, whether coaching women, mentoring girls or conversations with my daughters, I see how often we – girls *and* women – need to be reminded of how special we are. And that is why *I can't wait to help you get started.*

So, on behalf of the girl in your life, **THANK YOU** for choosing to be her champion.

♡ **Joan**

- Go at your own pace. Take any pressure off yourself to finish everything in a set amount of time. Remember, we are working to avoid the Perfectionist Trap, and role-model compassion towards ourselves!

- The main themes we cover are **Confidence**, **Ambition** and **Compassion**. Within these three parts of the book, you will explore subtopics that make the learning digestible and memorable.

- Within each chapter, you will find challenges which prompts you to find deeper connection and experimentation with your girl.

- Writing prompts like "Stop & Reflect" will help you absorb the topic, and reflect on your own perspective and experiences before you engage with your girl. There is also space at the end of each part for you to discuss your biggest takeaways together. (or doodle!)

Confidence

CHAPTER 1

Cultivate Confidence

Her small hand gripped mine as we approached the big, blue doors. Our family had moved to this town three days ago, and it was my seven-year-old daughter, Addie's, first day of school. I had rehearsed many encouraging things to say before she disappeared inside. I planned to tell her: "you are so great at making new friends", and "it's ok to feel lots of emotions", and remind her "I will be at the flag-pole as soon as school lets out!". My insides fluttered as Addie, my husband and I inched closer to the building. I knew Addie would pass through that blue door and into 2nd grade with zero friends because we had moved during a global pandemic. I knew no one would be there to greet her as a new student and, worst of all, she was wearing a mask that hid her cheerful smile.

But, before I could say a thing, Addie spun around to hug us and strode off with-out. Ever. Turning. Back. Sure enough, when we picked her up, she was fizzing with excitement over her new school, her kind teacher, and the new friends she had already made. Stunned, I asked her if she knew how brave she had been. I'll never forget her reply: "I'm confident I will try my best, and someone will care."

Fast-forward two years and this confident firecracker of a daughter feels like a distant memory. These days, nine-year-old Addie is navigating a steep confidence yo-yo of major lows and barely waist-level highs. It's as if someone emptied her confidence gas tank. What on earth happened?

As it turns out, Addie is not alone. Around the age of eight, girls' confidence takes its first noticeable – and steeply negative – decline. Research shows that their confidence plummets by 30% through age 14[1]. What's more, girls' anxiety rates have skyrocketed over the past ten years. Why? A variety of reasons. There's the 'curse of behaving like a good girl' (more on this later), and the addictive trap of perfectionism and people-pleasing tendencies, all of which are reinforced by the bombardment of negative images on social and mainstream media. Everything conspires to pressure girls to be perfect, and to compare their every move and body part to girls they know (or will never know). It is not until a woman is in her 40s that she matches a man's confidence levels, and then begins to outpace him. By her 50s, she never looks back!

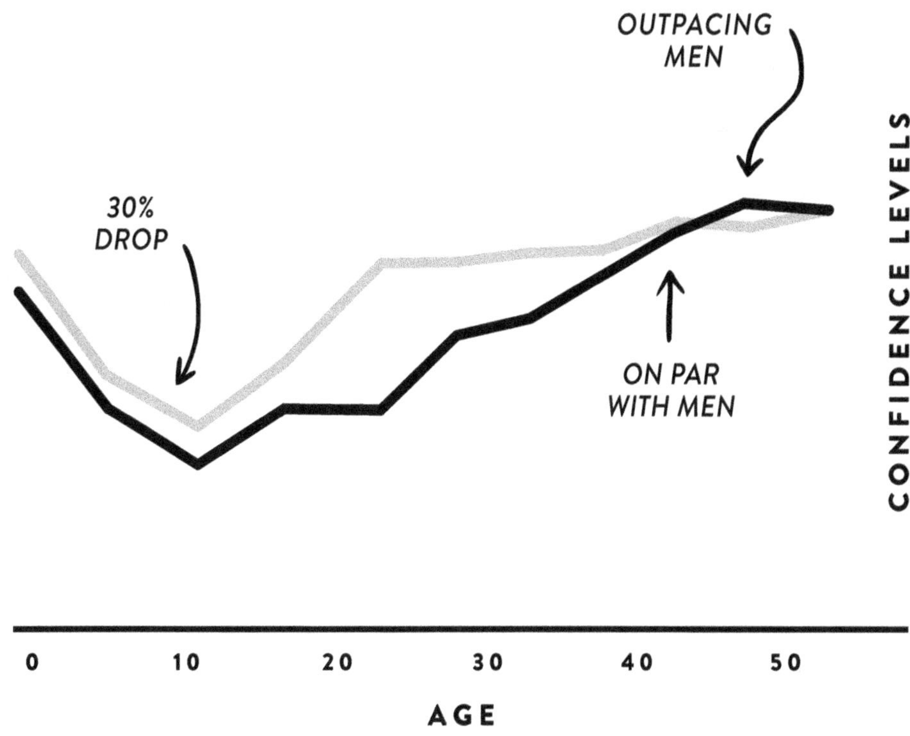

[1] *The Confidence Code* Katy Kay and Claire Shipman

Why should women wait 30+ years to feel enough?
How can we disrupt this cycle earlier before
the confidence rollercoaster begins?

GIRLS & CONFIDENCE

____

____

____

____

____

____

____

____

____

Tapping into your own confidence journey will prepare
you to guide and support your girl's reflections.

Take a moment to recall an early childhood memory when you felt confident and
brave enough to try something new. Use this space to visualize that moment.
Capture exactly what you did, and how it felt.

In 2018, I attended a middle school global girls' conference, where a 12-year-old girl shared her definition of confidence:

> "Self-confidence is the ability to be and do all that you want in the world… and be yourself in the process."

As the room furiously snapped their fingers in agreement, I yearned to speak up. But, I paused because deep down I knew this was a bigger conversation about the challenges that threatened that vision. The first part of this definition – *be and do all that you want in the world* – is empowering because it is grounded in pursuing one's potential and purpose. This should be encouraging to kids and teens. It is my hope and belief that everyone deserves to pursue one's potential. But the second part, about not having to change who we are to achieve our purpose? This gave me pause because I wanted them to be aware of the forces that could threaten their unique value and to avoid the pressures to diminish themselves.

What these girls didn't yet understand is a phenomena I've named the "conforming consequence." In my research on girls between the ages of 6-12, I was surprised to find that the majority of them struggle to remain authentic to their true selves. Why? Because they face a barrage of negative media, unhealthy social dynamics and biased cultural constraints. This trinity of negative pressure elevates negative self-talk like a bully in a girl's brain. It becomes almost impossible for her to quiet the noise and see herself, and her needs, clearly. The pressure to fit in, not to rock the boat, and not to stand out are right around the corner.

Over the years, I've developed my own definition of confidence. Modern self-confidence, the kind that breaks through the noise of perfectionism, hinges on the belief that you can do anything you set your mind to, and *deserve* to remain true to yourself in the journey to achieve your potential (stay true to your values, your style, and your uniqueness.)

confidence noun
con·fi·dence
> the belief that you can do anything you set your mind to, and *deserve* to remain true to yourself

It's why *Girls &*'s mission is to ensure that we empower women much earlier. We want to connect with them in girlhood, and teach them that <u>they</u> <u>are</u> <u>enough</u>. That everything girls bring to the table is **valued**, and deserves to be **seen** and **heard**.

And here's the great thing about confidence: you don't have to be born confident. Decades of research prove that it's a skill; a muscle you can grow with intention. Confidence is built by putting our thoughts (reflections and awareness) into action (micro-steps that make muscle memory). Throughout Part 1, I will explore experiences and barriers young girls face, then counter them with confidence-building exercises.

Over the next three chapters, we will delve into a series of **Challenges** ⚑ that provide step-by step guidance to support your conversations with your girl. The challenges will benefit both your girl and you, as her fierce advocate. Consider each of the following chapters building blocks in the foundation of cultivating her confidence. Together, we will question conventional thinking and antiquated expectations in order to empower girls to drive confidently toward their goals.

CHAPTER 2

Celebrate Her Strengths

At an early age, girls have access to their truest selves: the playful, creative, risk-taking, fearless, speak-your-mind selves. But, as we discussed earlier, society starts to pressure girls to give up their true selves, by charging at them with negative-biased messages on TV, in movies, commercials, print and digital publications, and, of course, social media. There may also be cultural and family influences that negatively shape a girl's sense of her self-worth and value in the world. Girls begin to worry more. Girls start to overthink about what others need, and how others think of them, instead of pushing back on the pressure to live up to someone else's expectations. The comparison culture bombards them with air-brushed images, and a wave of FOMO (fear of missing out) takes over.

"I'm the worst kid. No one thinks I'm good at anything," my five-year-old daughter, Juliette, cries out, unable to handle her intense emotions after a tough day in kindergarten. "All the other kids do everything right. The teachers love them, and I'm the bad one." Juliette's self-doubt was beginning to overwhelm her in social and home-life situations. She was in the habit of catastrophizing every mistake. Fear, anger, sadness and disappointment were stripping away Juliette's sweet, outgoing, and thoughtful self. Somehow the confidence crush we'd experienced with Addie was flooding my younger daughter at an earlier stage.

My husband and I felt we needed more tools and guidance so we contacted a school leader for help. This leader was amazing. She offered us several strategies to help Juliette navigate her emotions, but one, in particular, hit me hard. Looking at us across her desk, she asked: "How well does Juliette understand her strengths?" The crazy thing is, identifying and speaking up about strengths is an exercise I lead with professional women every week, and yet it had never occurred to me that I should try this with my own daughter. As modern 21st century parents, we assume we have more instincts and knowledge because we are flooded with nonstop advice and education. But it's far more information than we could ever consume, and we are only human. With all the best intentions, we can still be disconnected from what's happening right in front of us. We aren't alone in this, and it's a stark reminder of the critical value of community. More role models, helpers, advocates and champions for our girls strengthen our collective community. And we deserve to give ourselves grace as we navigate raising girls without a one-size-fits-all playbook. Once I'd got over the initial surprise, we discussed ways to build these encouraging conversations into rituals for Juliette, and repeat the exercises regularly in different environments.

So, where do we start? Start with her strengths. The first challenge is designed to illuminate your girl's unique value.

Own Her Strengths

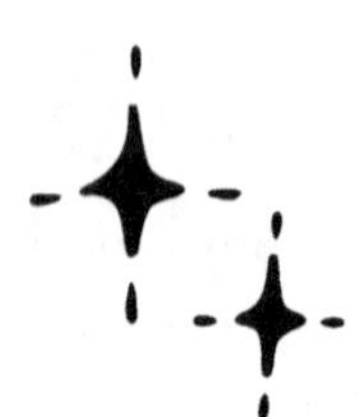

Research shows that girls and women do not spend enough time identifying – and speaking up about – their strengths. However, they spend plenty of time scrutinizing their weaknesses, and the areas in which they feel less than others. Let's flip that switch. Talk to your girl about her unique strengths. Help her recognize where she excels, and model this by sharing your strengths with her, too. Don't rush this! It may take several conversations to create a list of 6-8 strengths.

TIP: *For the "Own Her Strengths" challenge on the next page where you will work with her to list her strengths, make sure you also work on writing your own strengths down as well. Take time on the first column then come back to the second and third columns after you complete a couple strengths. For younger girls under age 9, you should come up with a list of possible strengths she can refer to which will help her identify which ones work for her.*

Use post-it notes or write on a separate piece of paper from the workbook to record the list of her strengths. Then encourage her to put this list somewhere she can see it daily – like on her nightstand, the refrigerator, or tape it to the bathroom mirror.

Ask her to look at the list every day for a set period, like one whole week. For younger girls, you could mention her strengths when you see them in action. Creating a ritual around looking at her strengths will make a profound impression on her memory, and ensure her strengths remain at the top of her mind throughout the day.

Own Her Strengths

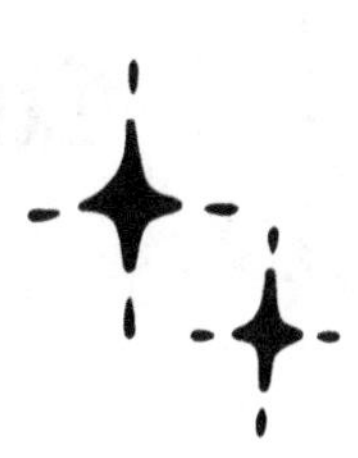

MY STRENGTH	HOW I USE IT	WHY IT GIVES ME ENERGY
thoughtful	*I made a good luck card for my sister before her soccer tryouts*	*I like helping others feel good*

Leverage Her Strengths

Now that you and your girl have taken time to list her strengths, and explore how they give her energy, let's put them to work! Owning her strengths gives your girl the ability to face challenges, and become more resilient and resourceful. Our goal in this exercise is to help her consider ways to use her strengths in different situations. This will help her feel empowered and confident that she can lean on her strengths in good times and tough ones, too.

Ask: What is the impact of your strength on others, and how do you know this? What feedback do you get from others about your strength?

Leverage Her Strengths

1. *Think about the activities or hobbies you enjoy the most. In what ways do these activities put your strengths to use?*

2. *Can you think of any new opportunities where you could use your strength?*

3. *Think about any activities or experiences you are looking forward to. How could your strengths be used to help you enjoy that experience?*

4. *Think about any activities or experiences you may be nervous or overwhelmed about. How could your strengths be used to help you navigate them and feel stronger?*

Support Her Strengths

When a girl learns to spot strengths, she will begin to see them everywhere. And she will begin to notice strengths in her friends, family, and other people she meets day to day. This helps her to develop positive personal interactions.

Have a conversation with her about how and why she noticed someone else's strengths. You can go a step further and ask her how she could share these kind observations with those people.

Encourage her to keep a journal, or come back to this section of the workbook when she has the opportunity to compliment someone's strengths or celebrate their achievements. She can record how she shows her appreciation for those people and helps them celebrate their strengths. The following exercise encourages her to celebrate others' strengths, which will help her see it's important to recognize her own.

Ask your girl to list three strengths
for each of the following people.

1. A close friend

____

____

____

2. A family member

____

____

____

3. Someone she admires

____

____

____

Record notes from your conversations to help explore her strengths. What went well? What was challenging?

GIRLS & CONFIDENCE

this" -alice P.
BE CONFIDE-
NT
(IOK)
BE CREATIVE
WORK
B

CHAPTER 3

Scrap.... Good Girl Pressure

Let's talk about the 'curse of the good girl'. Behaving like a good girl is associated with being a rule follower, exhibiting good manners, and staying away from mischief or high risk situations. It begins in early childhood, and is a socialized need to ask for permission instead of believing we have a *choice* in how we spend our time. We are always looking for approval and second-guessing our decisions and actions. We begin to notice patterns in how often women feel pressured to stifle their true emotions in an effort to keep the peace around them. Yet, emotions are powerful clues. The earlier in life we can teach a girl to view emotions as tools, the greater our chance to grow her confidence, and to teach her to balance others' needs while prioritizing her own. Above all, we want her to develop her 'core agency' – by which, I mean the feeling of control over her actions and their consequences.

Developing agency in girls between the ages of 8-12 will help them learn decision-making and conflict-management skills. Our efforts to encourage her to navigate her feelings in order to get clearer on what she wants out of a situation or relationship will build resilience and independence, as well. Experimenting with social skills will help your girl better communicate and express herself. Trust me, it will make a tremendous difference in preparing her for challenges that present in college and professional environments.

The 'curse of the good girl' begins in childhood and continues when we graduate college and enter the workplace. How does it manifest? By taking on roles like office secretary or 'office mother' when you are really the one in charge. Or it's not correcting a client who addresses male colleagues first in a meeting, even though you are the boss. Or it means being nice, but not too friendly; or becoming a people pleaser and a doormat. The societal pressure to be polite, coupled with women's historical lack of permission and skills to counter that perception, prevents us from claiming our authentic feelings and asserting ourselves. And so, women feel pressured to keep the peace, not to take things personally, and to put themselves – and their needs – last.

As a mother of two young daughters, this weighs on me constantly. I hope to raise my daughters with confidence, dignity, and good manners. But there is a fine line between having good manners, and being perceived as a 'good girl.'

When is behaving like 'a good girl' a curse,
and when is it a compliment?

What are your experiences with the pressure to be
polite, behave and be perceived as 'a good girl'?
How did this influence your decisions and behaviors?

____

____

____

____

____

____

____

____

Motherhood, and my internal struggles to be a leader who is both well-liked and respected, have been dual motivations that have driven my research over the past decade. I made it my mission to learn more about 'good girl thinking' and how it affects women in the workplace. I wanted to connect what girls learn from a young age to what professional women tell me in my research.

I discovered two key things:

1. Part of our struggle is a lack of skills and knowledge that would enable us to handle conflict, and to respond to situations that make us uncomfortable. 'Good girls' don't argue or act out, after all. Whether we are five years old or fifty, women aren't given the space or permission to assert themselves, nor advocate directly for what they want, nor resolve conflict openly without consequence, like boys and men. In many cultures and home environments, girls are taught to avoid drawing attention to themselves, and to prioritize humility. But here's the truth: we can be humble and firm simultaneously!

2. Learning how to navigate our emotions is a crucial life skill that takes practice. Feelings have power. We can teach girls to view feelings as data to help them create a healthier more equitable, innovative, and compassionate society, workplace, home life, and community. Spending time with Dr. Marc Brackett, international bestselling author of *Permission to Feel*, has taught me that our emotions largely determine our actions. His global movement, inside schools and communities, helps children learn how to define and navigate their feelings. Brackett's research explains there are no bad or good emotions. They are either helpful or unhelpful depending on your goal in a situation. He believes we can align certain behaviors to an emotion, and this will help us move toward an emotion we want to feel if we are in an emotional state that is not helping us.

A key takeaway from all this?

Learning to sit with discomfort is a skill that will ultimately help your girl learn both to advocate for herself, and build negotiation and conflict-management skills. If she practices the following challenges with you to help her avoid using weak language and own her voice, she will build foundational skills to navigate conflict and make decisions. This can start as early as 6 years old and the payoff will be huge.

The following two exercises will help her kick diminishing behaviors to the curb, and eliminate any language that shrinks her self-belief. The goal at the end of this is to strengthen your girl's communication style and fuel her confidence.

Our culture works hard to rob girls and women of their sense of agency. The definition of 'agency' is 'the feeling of control over actions and their consequences.' A girl who feels good about herself and trusts her opinions is much less susceptible to bullying, people-pleasing, and peer pressure.

CHALLENGE
Sorry, Not Sorry

This exercise will help curb the habit of over-apologizing. The pressure girls and women feel to be agreeable manifests as people-pleasing tendencies in uncomfortable situations and, ultimately, becomes a habit even when we have nothing to be sorry for. This is entirely different from our ability to offer sincere and meaningful apologies. People make mistakes all the time. If we hurt someone, they deserve a heartfelt apology. But, far too often, our apologizing becomes a habitual reaction to uncomfortable or awkward situations.

Step 1

Discuss moments when you, as a grownup, lean on "I'm sorry" without reason. Examples like when someone runs into you, but you say "Sorry" to them. Or you want to jump into a conversation and say, "Sorry, but can I share an idea?". Or you didn't hear someone's last comment, so you say, "Sorry, can you repeat that for me." Try to explain to your girl how we have been socialized to over-apologize, even when we have done nothing wrong. The over-apologetic language diminishes our confidence and weakens our influence. Take notes on this conversation, as well as your girl's observations and opinions.

Sorry, Not Sorry

Step 2

Now replace the apologies with gratitude statements and other more assertive communication phrases.

When your teacher or classmate points out a mistake or misunderstanding:

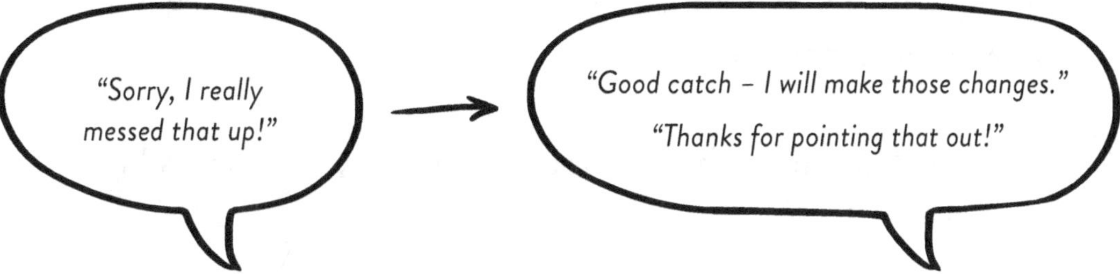

If a teammate tells you that you didn't pass the ball to them enough in the last game:

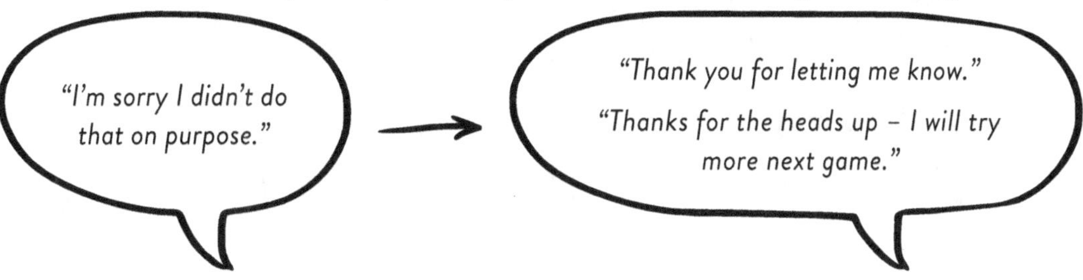

For children under the age of eight, you may want to gently remind them that they only have to say sorry once if it comes from the heart. They made a mistake, but they are not a mistake themselves.

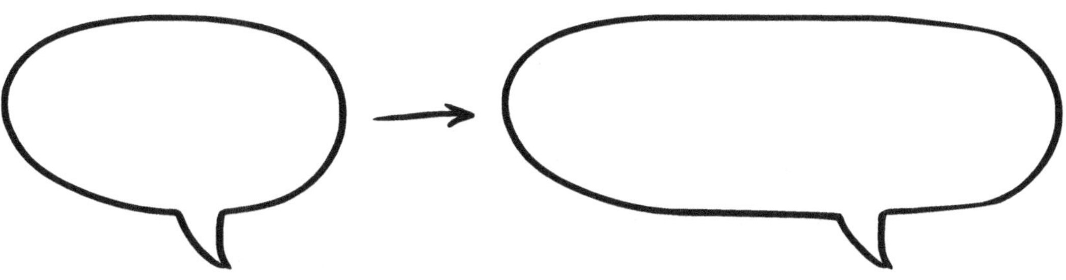

There are two parts to this exercise. First, show her this list of the most common 'filler language' and explain how it diminishes the power of our voice and presence when overused. Research shows that girls and women often lean on these words to hedge their ideas, preventing them from confidently stating their views or opinions[2].

Ask her if she uses these phrases or has any more to add to the list

✗ *"Oh," "Um," "Like," "Really," "You know".*

✗ *"This may be a stupid question."*

✗ *"This may sound silly."*

✗ *"I'm sure you are busy, but would it be ok if..."*

✗ _______________________________________

✗ _______________________________________

✗ _______________________________________

These diminishing statements undermine her self-respect before she has even offered her perspective. It is like telling the room, "Hey, I don't even think my voice or idea is that great, so don't bother paying attention to me."

[2] https://daily.jstor.org/totally-destructive-yet-oddly-instructive-speech-patterns-young-women/

Own Her Voice

Part two of this challenge is learning how to rephrase statements so that they have a stronger impact, and to help you navigate challenging conversations and situations.

Practice saying this, not that, to help your girl own her voice.

INSTEAD OF	→	SAY
"I think I am good at…"	→	*"My strength is…"*
"Why don't we try…"	→	*"Let's try…" or "My idea is…"*
"I feel like we should…"	→	*"We should…" or "Let's do this…"*
	→	
	→	
	→	

CHALLENGE

Speaking Up
& Self-Advocacy

Speaking up with confidence, honesty and respect is called being *assertive*. Here are some statements to help you practice advocating for yourself, your ideas, and your opinions. Use these words or messages to create a moment of pause to decide if you should walk away, stand up for yourself, or redirect the conversation. If someone says something that hurts your feelings, is talking about someone behind their back, or makes a comment that does not sit well with you, buy yourself some time.

Say:

"Ouch."

"Wow."

"That's your opinion."

"That doesn't make sense."

"That is none of my business."

"I don't like it when…"

I trust myself.

I can learn from
my mistakes,
but I am not a mistake.

I can learn and grow.

My emotions are mine.
They are not bad or good.
They are helpful or
unhelpful in a situation.

CHAPTER 4

Nurture Self-Trust

Trust is a critical factor in relationships. It impacts our everyday interactions, and is the backbone for remaining vigilant when advocating for ourselves. Studies have shown that, even more than trusting others, we must teach girls to trust themselves. Self-trust is crucial when it comes to navigating peer pressure and stress in their teen years into adulthood.

How do we define 'self-trust'? The Oxford English Dictionary defines it as: *The ability to believe and have faith in oneself and our abilities.* Without self-trust, a girl will begin to second-guess her decisions, which leads to pervasive self-doubt.

You may find she talks openly about a friendship that is frustrating her, or making her feel anxious, in an effort to protect or prepare herself for a situation. Or she may share that she isn't a hugger, and allows herself to express limits on the physical nature of any relationship. Both are common scenarios where girls need to trust their own judgement, instincts or abilities.

This is a three-step trust exercise I've used for over a decade with women and girls of all ages. The goal is to reinforce our belief that we can make good decisions for ourselves and withstand pressure to conform.

1. **Encourage her to listen to her instincts.** It's important to teach her to listen to her gut, not the bully in her brain that can say negative things. Talk through recent decisions she made that were hard – and those that were easy – to explore how she problem-solves. Compliment her on her thought-process more than the outcomes in her stories. Refer to page 43 for statements you can use to encourage her.

2. **Listen to her stories with intention.** This can be so much harder than it sounds. As parents, we are ready to help at a moment's notice, especially when we yearn to protect our children from pain. When expressing her feelings and telling her stories, we must stop thinking and listen. This validates her experiences, feelings, and thoughts. It validates that she matters.

3. Create space without judgment. Explore the power behind allowing her to disagree, express a difference in opinion, and speak her mind openly without judgment. Encouraging your girl to express herself and speak comfortably, and openly with you can increase her comfort in speaking up in other situations. Try asking her about general topics to engage her opinion, such as: "If a family gets a pet, who should be responsible for taking care of it?" or "What if your school had assigned seating for lunch in the cafeteria, how would this be helpful or not for students?" This could encourage her to think of a personal topic she wants to explore with you.

GIRLS & CONFIDENCE

Supportive statements to say to your girl:

"That sounds hard."

"It seems like you really listened to your own feelings."

"I'm proud of you for following your gut and staying true to your feelings."

Examples for encouraging difference of opinion:

"That is a fair point. I'm glad you explained your perspective to me."

"I see where you are coming from."

"Thank you for sharing that with me so I can better understand how you see what happened."

I deserve
to take breaks.

My future
is positive.

Mistakes
are necessary.

I am aware
of this moment.

I am trustworthy.

I have
good intentions.

I can make healthy
decisions and choices.

3 KEY BUILDING BLOCKS
to Cultivate Confidence
1
2 3

Celebrate Her Strengths

Scrap..... Good Girl Pressure

Nurture Self-Trust

Confidence Reflection

Use this space to record notes and reflections,
as well as the ways you interacted with your girl.

Research shows that we can increase our propensity to problem-solve through free drawing, and putting our ideas into images on paper without rigid constraint.

Use this space to draw a reflection of the **Confidence** chapters, and your interactions with your girl.

Our Game Plan

Use this space to write out your commitments to growing your confidence together. Refer to the challenges and exercises that inspired you most, and note how you will turn to them – and each other – when you need a confidence boost.

CONFIDENCE RESOURCES

● ● ● ●

♥ Organizations/Initiatives

- *LiveGirl* is a Connecticut-based nonprofit organization that builds confident, inclusive leaders. Their mission is to equip the next generation of diverse, brave female leaders with skills, community, and connections, so that ALL girls may thrive and make a positive impact on the world. *LiveGirl* serves thousands of girls in grades 5 through college age, annually, in free-of-charge innovative leadership development and mentoring programs, such as the eight-week Confidence Clubs, Annual Summits and Summer Camps. **golivegirl.org**

- *Girls Leadership* non-profit teaches girls to exercise the power of their voice through programs grounded in social-emotional learning. They provide programs for girls, workshops for families, and professional-development training for teachers, guidance counselors, and non-profit staff. My daughter, Addison, and I had a strong, positive experience participating in their in-person and virtual trainings series: *Girl & Her Grownup*. **girlsleadership.org**

- *Girls Inc.* (national and local chapters) is building the new generation of strong, smart, and bold leaders through direct service and advocacy. Through the *Girls Inc. Experience*, professionally-trained staff and volunteers provide mentorship, safe spaces, and programming that address the unique challenges girls face, and are proven to help girls succeed. They cultivate safe environments where girls are encouraged to take risks, learn from experiences, and grow. *Girls Inc.* works with – and for – girls to advocate for policies to overcome the social and systemic barriers that threaten their ability to succeed. **girlsinc.org**

▌ Books

- *Under Pressure* by Lisa Damour
- *Enough As She Is* by Rachel Simmons
- *Strong is the New Pretty* by Kate T. Parker
- *Play Like A Girl* by Kate T. Parker

☰ Articles

- **"How Puberty Kills Girls' Confidence"** by Claire Shipman, Katty Kay, and JillEllyn Riley. *The Atlantic*, September 2018
- **"The State of Girls' Mental Health and Self-Confidence, in charts"** by Caitlynn Peetz. *Edweek.org*, November 2023

♫ Podcast Episodes

- **Raising Good Humans with Dr. Aliza Pressman podcast** – Season 3, Ep 20: *The Price Women Pay to Be Good with Elise Loehnen*
- **Raising Good Humans with Dr. Aliza Pressman podcast** – Season 2, Ep 97: *Your Daughter Has Superpowers with Donna Jackson Nakazawa*

▶ Video Links

- **SheBelieves Summit: Breaking Barriers Panel – Leaders in Sport.** A panel of remarkable women working in sports including: Aly Wagner, American sports broadcaster and two-time gold medalist; Crystal Dunn, Defender for U.S. Women's National Soccer Team; Katayoun Khosrowyar, Head Coach for Iran's U-19 Girls' Soccer National Team; Ibtihaj Muhammad, U.S. Olympic Medalist, and Katie Sowers, Offensive Assistant Coach, San Francisco 49ers, who became the first female (and first openly-gay) coach in a Super Bowl.
- **Strong is The New Pretty by Kate T. Parker.** Parker shares her inspiration behind creating her photo book, "Strong is the New Pretty." She hopes that this idea will transform the way we think about beauty standards.
- **The Confidence Crisis for Girls: What Adults Need to Know and Do.** Dr. Shekyra Decree discusses the big things adults need to know about girls' confidence with easy action steps to follow.
- **My Identity is a Superpower by America Ferrera.** In this TEDTalk, actor, director and activist America Ferrera calls for more authentic representation of different cultures in media, and a shift in how we tell our stories.

PART Two

Ambition

CHAPTER 5

The New Ambition Equation

Saira began doodling and writing out her thoughts as early as age six. She used crayons, markers, felt tip pens, and anything available to bring her ideas and dreams to life on paper. In 2nd grade, during a class project, a classmate made fun of Saira's drawings and called them "babyish" and "weird". This was enough to make Saira want to hide her work and shy away from ever sharing it publicly. Thankfully, a few weeks later, Saira's teacher praised an essay she wrote about her favorite book and encouraged her to submit it to a local library contest. She suggested Saira make her work stand out by illustrating her favorite parts in the side bar of the essay. Although she didn't win the contest, Saira and her family were proud to visit the wall of contestants in the library, and see her work displayed for the community. Several years later, Saira had the courage to submit to a statewide competition where she wrote a reflection piece about how her teacher's recognition, and encouragement of her passion, sparked her ambition and refueled her confidence to pursue more ways to express it.

ambition noun

am·bi·tion

> a strong desire to do or to achieve something,
> typically requiring determination and hard work

Ambition gets a bad rap. It's often negatively associated with ruthless quests for fame, fortune and power. But I'm here to tell you that ambition can be a force for good. However, in order to make ambition work for girls, we need to move away from the standard definition above and completely rebrand it. Before we get onto that, let's tackle three key myths about ambition...

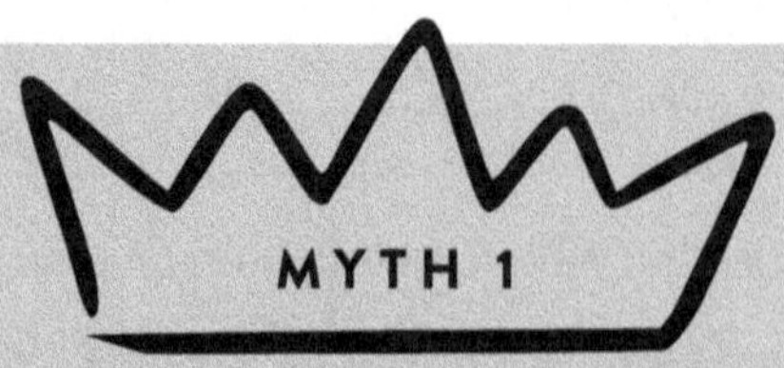

Girls are not as ambitious as boys. Commonly referred to as the "Ambition Gap".

Research studies published between 2005-2023 continue to reveal that in childhood, girls are clear and energized about their ambitions. A recent nationally-representative U.S. poll of 1,000 children and adolescents ages 10 to 19 found that girls were slightly more likely than boys to say being a leader was a very important life goal, and three-quarters of girls said having a successful career was very important. Their goals are ambitious, even limitless, and they make no apologies for pursuing them. We love hearing this!

The "Ambition Gap" is the theory that gender inequities in the workplace exist because women are simply less ambitious than men, and many assume this starts in childhood. While this narrative is outdated, it needs attention because it's falsely used to justify pay, wealth, and leadership gaps. Research, and my decade of experience leading global training for women in the workforce, prove this wrong. We have proof that women do ask for more – more money, greater responsibilities – and are committed and loyal to their organization's goals. In one study, 990 participants who graduated from business school between 2015 and 2019 were asked a series of questions about their job search, the essential one being, "Did you negotiate your job offer?" Fifty-four percent of women reported negotiating offers compared to 44% of men, contradicting the idea that women don't negotiate. Yet, while women do pursue advanced education, training, and actively pursue negotiation, we still have not closed the gender pay gap. Worldwide, women only make 77 cents for every dollar earned by men. As a result, there's a lifetime of income inequality impacting women's earning potential and long-term financial stability.

Bottom line, girls <u>are</u> ambitious. Women <u>do</u> pursue high-paying careers <u>and</u> seek out leadership opportunities. The impression that ambition wanes over time as she ages is not the right story. We need to understand ambition and how the environment girls and women encounter when pursuing ambition plays a role.

When it comes to childhood ambitions, there are two distinct factors in place: the **mastery of a special skill** (🎨, 🎻, ⚽, 🏀, 🛼) and **recognition for it** (🏆, 🏅, 👏, 🖼, 👍). Most learning cycles follow a path where recognition fuels the next stage of learning. Imagine your eight-year-old self dreaming of becoming a famous ballerina or an astronaut on the first mission to Saturn. You take ballet classes, or study space, and put your heart into learning the skills associated with these big dreams. Then someone recognizes you – a coach, a teacher, a community contest judge, or a recital audience. Suddenly you feel (and absorb) credible praise. This cycle fuels early ambitions.

What does this teach us? That ambition is not a fixed trait. It's not something you simply lose or grow out of, but is nurtured or damaged by your environment. While boys and men are praised and rewarded for their ambitions, girls and women are far more likely to be penalized and judged for assertive or aggressive behaviors. This is called the **Likeability Penalty.**

Have you heard about The Tallest Poppy? It's the first international study of its kind that looks at thousands of working women across 103 countries, from all demographics and professions. The study's goal? To determine how women's mental health, wellbeing, engagement and performance are affected by interactions with their clients, colleagues, and leaders in regard to their success and accomplishments. An astounding 86.8% indicated that at some point in their career, either past or present, they have experienced hostility or have been penalized and/or ostracized because of their success or achievements. The form of attacks experienced by women are broad and far-reaching – from being undermined or excluded, to experiencing microaggressions and belittling, to having their achievements downplayed. This study showcases the negative impact of the "likeability penalty", a deep rooted bias that is rooted in expectations. We expect men to be more assertive, so when they lead or act assertive it feels natural. We expect women to be kind and communal, so when they assert themselves or express ambition, we (both men and women) like them less. **The next step is change, and it must come quickly, beginning with the celebration of, and respect for, girls' and women's ambitions.**

Now that we have dispelled myths about girls and women not being as ambitious as boys and men, we can credibly ask: does the Ambition Gap even exist? Or could this be an excuse that avoids taking a more critical look at the bias and the negative reactions towards successful and assertive girls and women? Take a moment and reflect on the Likeability Penalty and any experiences you have had that relate to this topic.

GIRLS & AMBITION

Let's explore ambition for your girl and if the environment around her played a role. Think back to a specific skill your girl has mastered, and was recognized for. Can you list three ways it impacted her confidence, and her desire to pursue it?

____

____

____

____

____

____

____

____

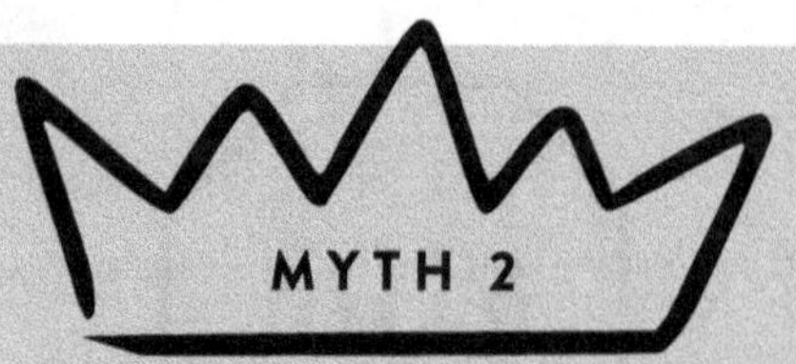

Perfection is
the path to success.

Girls mistake perfection for ambition, believing it's the *only* route to success. Setting sky-high unrealistic expectations of themselves, they believe working the hardest, with no room for mistakes, is the singular path to achieving all their goals. It's exhausting, and it's no secret that girls and women identify as perfectionists more than boys and men, as they strive to be perfect in every role they play. Perfect Daughter, Perfect Sister, Perfect Student, Perfect Teammate. This persists into adulthood with the pressure of being the perfect professional, perfect mother, perfect wife, etc. We set lofty and loaded expectations upon ourselves; when we don't hit them, the tumble is vertical and toxic. Girls learn way too young to be critical of themselves every step of the way, leaving no room for self-compassion over mistakes. This is when guilt, shame and envy spike, threatening to derail their ambition and confidence. Our goal is to separate this perfection problem from ambition and achievement earlier in a girl's life.

Have you struggled with the **Perfectionist Trap**, and the pressure to excel at everything by setting unrealistic goals on yourself? How has it impacted your personal sense of achievement (the ability to own your success and take credit for your hard work)? Did you deflect praise? Does this internal pressure impact your ambition, and leave you second-guessing yourself before going after a goal?

Now think about your girl. Have you observed the same self-critical behaviors in her? Does she hold herself to any unrealistic goals and pressures?

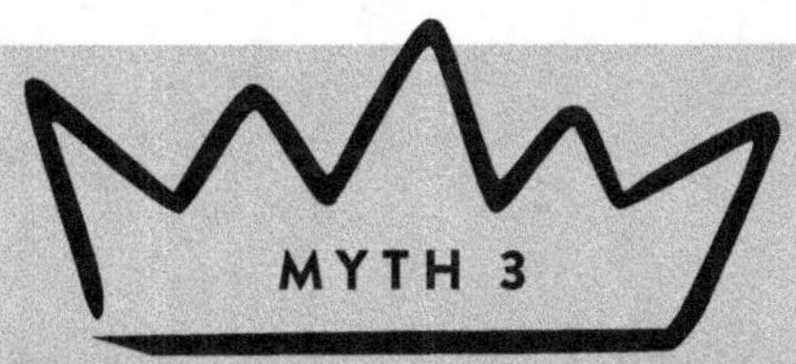

Girl Power is enough.

The "girl power" message tells girls they can *be* and *do* anything. While this message is empowering, it doesn't equip girls with honest preparation for the stubborn gender inequalities they will face. We all know that education and work ethic are two crucial ingredients for success. In the United States, women have been earning more bachelor degrees than men for four decades, yet women remain underrepresented in senior leadership in almost every industry. So why is this not moving the needle fast enough in the leadership representation and power dynamics needed to solidify equity?

"What we realized is that, in order to really get to equality in leadership everywhere, from our parliaments to our statehouses to our homes, we're going to have to go younger," Sheryl Sandberg, author of global bestseller, *Lean In*, said in an interview with The Associated Press. "Who wants to say to a girl seven years before she enters the workforce, 'One day you're going to be in a meeting and some man is going to talk over you, voice something you just said and get credit for your ideas,'" Sandberg asked. "We don't want to tell our daughters that."

But speaking about those biases, Sandberg continued allows for a conversation about how to counteract them. "We're going to start telling you the challenges, but then we're also going to equip you, and the people around you, to change them."

Numerous organizations work tirelessly to champion girls' access to education, which literally saves lives in many parts of the world. But education is one thing, preparing them with **mentorship** and **sponsorship** to enter male-dominated fields and build long-term careers is another critical element.

mentorship noun
men·tor·ship
    someone who teaches, guides, advises and offers direction to someone less experienced

sponsorship noun
spon·sor·ship
    someone in a position of power who actively advocates for you, puts your name forward for high-stakes assignments that win notice and promotion, and spends their political capital at work in your name

Superhuman work ethic is often mistaken for perfectionism. Girls and women are taught to sacrifice too much personal time to perform perfectly. The "put your head down, work hard, and don't make waves" advice shrinks a girl's self-advocacy and backfires when she enters the world of work where relationships and advocating for yourself are vital. Even with our noble intentions to empower, Girl Power messaging is not enough. We can tell girls they can *be* and *do* anything, which is <u>essential</u>, but we also need to unearth and <u>speak openly and honestly</u> about the biased barriers – such as The Likeability Penalty – standing in their way.

Gender inequity is not a thing of the past, and without a heads up, girls end up blaming themselves when they face bias or unfair treatment, leading them to internalize harmful stereotypes.

Take a moment to think about all the messages we encounter day-to-day in the media, our homes, our schools, and through our daily interactions. What messages have influenced your personal and professional journey (positive and negative)? What messages is your girl exposed to in her day-to-day interactions? Have you seen it impact her behaviors, decisions, outlook or view of herself and others (girls and boys)?

____

____

____

____

____

____

____

After facilitating multi-day training programs with thousands of women between 2019-2023, I saw a clear and urgent need to rebrand ambition for modern women. I went through hundreds of chat transcripts, reviewed 60+ pre-and post-training surveys from my global programs, and sifted through all my participant notes on what women felt were their biggest barriers and greatest enablers of success. Finally, I was able to distill my findings into three empowering traits that redefine ambition through a female lens.

Here is my new ambition equation:

$$\frac{\text{Purpose} + \text{Values} + \text{Self-Advocacy}}{} = \text{Ambition}$$

Let me explain.

Purpose

All my research has shown that purpose is a more dominant driver than ego or power, and is far more appealing to girls and women. Ample research has shown that identifying and pursuing a purpose improves individuals' physical and mental wellbeing. Power, wealth and fame are certainly alluring at earlier ages, but the flashy façade fades fast, whereas purpose, impact and meaning soar as key drivers during girlhood and womanhood.

Values

Research shows that girls link power to their gender less often than boys. However, they can be as motivated if the goal is aligned with their values. For men, power is viewed as a zero-sum game (aka one person's gain is another person's loss), but this conflicts with women's strong desires to collaborate and connect. Girls and women want the "power to do" something; boys and men tend to want "power over" something or someone. However, 21st-century leadership research proves that leaders today must be empowered with high humility, resilience, and self-awareness; far different from the old ways of emphasizing command-and-control leadership styles in hierarchical relationships. In today's digital, globally-connected world, teams rely on collaborative, inclusive leaders to help them contribute to their fullest. This is all good news for girls who value purpose, impact, and meaning.

Self-Advocacy

Yet, with all this good news about the synergy between what the world needs and what girls are ready to contribute, we still encounter bias on the journey to equality. Girls will face pushback when they take the lead, speak up or advocate for themselves and their ideas, essentially putting their ambition into action. So, we must teach them how to become their own best advocate to sustain their confidence and courage when their ambition is inevitably assaulted by bias and stereotype. The building blocks of ambition will help us be honest with our girls so they are motivated to embrace their ambitions, identify unfair treatment, and collaborate with others to drive toward their goals and lead authentically.

CHAPTER 6

Push Back on Perfection

A girl who exhibits healthy striving behaviors fueled by self-confidence and self-worth is our goal, NOT perfection.

Here's the deal. Perfection only exists in our minds! Think about it: our version of perfection will always be different from someone else's, yet we mistakenly hold ours up as the absolute vision. It is a total trap. The Perfectionist Trap! It holds us back from taking risks, learning from mistakes, and celebrating any progress we make. Perfection goes hand-in-hand with people-pleasing. And, this may come as a surprise, but perfection's best friend is procrastination. All this inner pressure to be perfect can overwhelm us from getting started on our goals as we procrastinate or delay taking action. Ultimately, perfectionism isolates us from others and can put us in a position to feel less worthy than those around us.

overthinking verb
over·think·ing
> when you put too much time into thinking about
> or analyzing something in a way that is more harmful
> than helpful

ruminating verb
ru·mi·nate·ing
> a style of coping that is repetitive thinking or dwelling
> on negative feelings and distress and their causes and
> consequences

Look out for these: overthinking and ruminating.

You'll see these behaviors surface after tough times in school, sports or activities, friend interactions, and social conversations. She may begin overanalyzing to understand past experiences better, and gain clarity over future situations and decisions. But, sometimes, these behaviors surface because of her fear of not being in control, feeling overwhelmed, or a fear of making the wrong decision or taking risks. She begins replaying every event or situation over and over in her head and second-guessing or **overthinking** her actions and decisions. She may start **ruminating** and replaying a conversation or situation in the past repeatedly, continually worrying about what she did or said. The earlier we step in to teach her why this trap is detrimental to her wellbeing, the more likely she will be to sidestep it, and focus on meaningful, realistic goals.

Picture a nine-year-old girl walking home from school after taking a challenging math test. "I think I got 100% on my test. I hope I did. I must have. But, maybe I didn't. Maybe I messed up that word problem, or my teacher will take away points because I got the bonus problem wrong. She said something last week about how hard it is to read my handwriting sometimes. I definitely think she won't be able to read my work on the test. Oh no, she is going to say something in front of the whole class, and everyone will know my work is sloppy and fail me on the test!"

As Reshma Saujani, founder of *Girls Who Code* and author of *Brave Not Perfect* says, "Girls and women are marred by perfection. It conditions us to go so quickly from, 'I made a typo', to 'I'm dumb, I'm stupid, oh my God I'm gonna get fired,' all in, like, ten seconds!" That's the behavior we are trying to help girls and women unlearn. We need to help her put on the breaks when that spiral of negative thinking takes over her brain, so she can change the channel to a more positive, productive mindset.

When is "Good Enough" Enough?

In this exercise, you will work with your girl to strengthen her problem-solving and decision-making skills so she can push back on perfection.

Step 1

Explain the concept of "good enough". "Good enough" doesn't mean bad or poor quality. The principle of "good enough" is this: identify the point past which putting more resources (time, effort or money) into something won't improve it in a meaningful manner, so you should move on. It means that if, after two hours' work on a 5th-grade writing assignment, the work is 95% as good as it would be after five hours' work, then 95% is good enough, so you should move on.

NOTES

____

____

____

____

When is "Good Enough" Enough?

Step 2

Reflect on a recent situation where your girl struggled when spending a tremendous amount of time working toward a goal or completing a task. Use this situation reflection to talk through three ways to be "good enough" that could have saved her time or effort.

1. **Clear:** Clear goals can help you set boundaries and time limits. Walk through the situation, explore her goals, and be clear about identifying them. Then help her see that her work doesn't have to be perfect to achieve them.

2. **Fear:** Ask her what she is afraid of when finishing her work at the 'good enough' point, and then discuss her fears to see if they're unsupported and unrealistic.

3. **Dear:** Consider what else she could be doing with the extra time and effort spent going past the 'good enough' point. Give her a chance to really weigh the cost of missing out on these other activities that are near and dear to her heart and happiness. Is perfect worth it?

CHAPTER 7

Learn to Fail Forward!!

It's impossible to truly live without failing at something.

In 2008, J.K. Rowling (bestselling author of the *Harry Potter* series) spoke to the benefits of failure to the graduating class at Harvard. "Failure taught me things about myself that I could have learned no other way. The knowledge that you have emerged wiser and stronger from setbacks means that you are, ever after, secure in your ability to survive. You will never truly know yourself or the strength of your relationships until both have been tested by adversity. Such knowledge is a true gift, for all that it is painfully won, and it has been worth more than any qualification I ever earned."

Let's help girls embrace failure by teaching them how to use an entrepreneurial mindset. The Girl Scout Entrepreneurship Report published in 2019 found that **six in ten girls have an entrepreneurial mindset**. The research found that "the social and emotional qualities that lead to successful entrepreneurship, like curiosity, confidence, and innovation, are also crucial for all types of academic and career success." If confidence is the motion of putting your thoughts into action (Part 1), entrepreneurs exemplify this by running with their ideas and turning them into action. This motion of pursuing new and different paths or ideas, without letting fear hold you back from trying, are essential life and business skills.

CASE STUDY

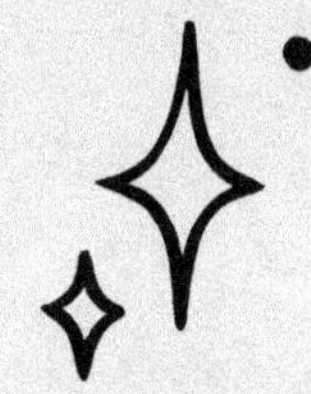

Abigail spotted her teacher backstage and burst into tears. "I failed! I forgot my whole dance!" she cried. He helped Abigail take a few calming breaths, and gently reminded her about all the work she had put in to make it to this very moment.

Abigail had been taking dance classes since she was four years old, and had blossomed in her annual recitals. Now ten, Abigail decided to challenge herself by performing a solo routine in a regional competition. The decision to compete alone was not made lightly. Although nervous, Abigail was hopeful that she could accomplish this milestone. Over the next few months, she focused on learning the routine, and diligently practicing at home. Abigail's parents and sister enthusiastically cheered her on, encouraging her to enjoy the experience.

The day before the competition, Abigail packed her sparkly costume and jazz shoes. She got a good night's rest, and ate a healthy breakfast. Both her body and brain were ready to perform!

When the time finally came, Abigail was ready to hit the stage. The lights went down and the music began. But, as Abigail turned to face the audience, she froze! She couldn't remember a single move. Panicking, she ran off stage.

As Abigail poured her heart out to her teacher, she had a moment to catch her breath. She listened as he told her that she was not a failure. That the most important thing was not to give up on herself. The competition allowed competitors a second chance if this was their first solo performance.

Abigail made the brave decision to try again. Composing herself, she returned to the stage. This time, when the music started, she focused on staying present. Tuning in to the steps she had worked so hard to prepare, Abigail performed her routine flawlessly. The pride she felt when the music stopped filled her entire body with a renewed sense of confidence. At the awards ceremony, Abigail placed 3rd and was praised for her courage. For Abigail, the lesson she learned about channeling her motivation, and showing herself grace under pressure, meant even more than the medal.

Overcome the Fear of Failure

Let's challenge girls in ways that channel their desire for creativity, and their aptitude for risk-taking into opportunities to fail. Ultimately this will help them learn how to overcome their fear of failure. When working with girls, don't just recognize their finished product or project, but celebrate and encourage them when they persist through challenges and setbacks along the way!

Nelson Mandela, former President of South Africa once said, "I never lose. I either win, or I learn."

Step 1

Explain to your girl that everyone fails. Begin by offering a story about a time when you failed. Model how to handle frustration and disappointment so she can take cues from you. Think out loud and let her listen to you solve a problem. Demonstrate how you are working to find a solution. Then ask her to take a turn sharing a story of when she did not achieve a desired goal, or faced a challenge. When you see that she is struggling or having a hard time, empathize with her. Be sure not to brush off her feelings. Try using language like, "I know you're really disappointed and that you wanted to do better."

Step 2

Teach your girl a lesson about how failure leads to resiliency and a growth mindset. Using her example, talk through what went wrong and look out for "all or nothing" language such as "I always…" or "I never…". Help her develop problem-solving skills by thinking through possible solutions, or different ways she could have approached the challenge to help her create a plan for next time. Encourage her to focus on reframing a situation and praise her effort in trying to do so. Remind your child to use this failure as a learning experience and try again. Recognizing this as a skill, and encouraging her to reflect and try again reinforces her effort more than the failure or the outcome itself. If at first you don't succeed, try again!

Being present counters the pitfalls of perfectionism because you are focused on enjoying and being in the moment. **Simply making the time to have these conversations, and deeply listen to her experiences and opinions, makes a difference.** Help her to stay present instead of agonizing over the future or ruminating over mistakes or tough moments in the past.

Overcome the Fear of Failure

Step 3

Start a ritual to celebrate failure. Failures grow your brain! When kids understand the brain science behind why mistakes improve learning, it's easy to get them excited about the possibilities. Introduce the idea of "Failure Fridays", which could be a day of the week when you read about a famous person who failed, or you share a story with each other about failing forward that past week.

A recent study published in *Developmental Cognitive Science* revealed that after making a mistake, children with growth mindsets show a larger brain response than those with fixed mindsets. They are also more likely to *improve their performance* as a result.

Failure is inevitable, but we can teach our girls to approach problem-solving and decision-making with a growth mindset.

Girls who are still developing their entrepreneurial mindset need the most support when it comes to conquering this fear. Being afraid to fail or try something new requires intentional coaching and encouragement from the people they trust.

I am worthy and
valuable, regardless
of my achievements.

Progress is more
important than
perfection.

I can learn and grow
from my challenges.

CHAPTER 8

Prime Her for Power

Give your girl permission to be powerful from within.

As discussed earlier, girls and women view power differently to boys and men. They are driven by purpose, impact, and meaning, so we want to encourage this view by giving her permission to be powerful from within, while reimagining the pursuit of power.

Eighty-two percent of girls want to positively impact society through their work, and nearly <u>all</u> want a future workplace where employees are treated fairly and paid equally, regardless of gender. Learning about examples of female leaders who leveraged the power of their positions and actions to create a positive impact will be memorable and meaningful for your girl. Share these stories in the context of teaching her how to express her purpose and how to set impact goals. The following challenge helps her connect her values to opportunities where she could grow her influence (and, therefore, power).

> **JULIETTE'S PURPOSE STATEMENT (AGE 6)**
> *I value kindness, being a good listener and helping. I care about animals and being a good sister. I hope to make a positive difference by having a caring heart with my friends and looking out for animals.*

Permission to Pursue Power with Purpose

Step 1

Help your girl to write a purpose statement. A purpose statement is a creative way to express the impact you hope to have in your lifetime inspired by your values and passions. It can be a compass to provide motivation and direction. Write your own purpose statement first so you can give her an example of how you connect your values and passions to having an impact in your lifetime.

Follow these steps below and complete the mad libs style purpose statement together.

1. *List your top 3 values. Offer examples like "Family, Community, Faith, Fairness..."*

2. *List your interests and passions, such as "playing a musical instrument or volunteering"*

3. *Finish this sentence: "If I could change something in the world, I would..."*

4. *Complete this purpose statement (example on pg. 80):*
   I value _______, _______ and _______. I care about _______ and _______. I hope to make a positive difference by ____________________.

Permission to Pursue Power with Purpose

Step 2

Discuss stories of women who have used their power and influence to drive change, lead for good, and make a meaningful impact. *Are there any examples in your personal life or local community that you could highlight?* The content that girls watch and read impacts their lives and ambitions. The stories we are told and the images that surround us in the media (TV, movies, print, and digital), play a critical role in shaping girls' and young women's aspirations.

Show her that *she-ro* stories are everywhere!

NOTES

____

____

____

____

____

Powerful books, TV series and movies that feature strong girls and women:

BOOKS	TV SERIES	DOCS FOR GROWN UPS
Juno Valentine *A is for Awesome* **EVA CHEN**	*Rosie Revere, Engineer; Ada Twist, Scientist*	*Angel City*
She Persisted (sports edition) **CHELSEA CLINTON**	*Izzy's Koala World*	*Girl Rising*
Little Leaders: Bold Women in Black History **VASHTI HARRISON**	*Jane*	*Miss Representation*
Malala's Magic Pencil **MALALA YOUSAFZAI**	*Nella the Princess Knight*	*He Named Me Malala*
Women in Science: 50 Fearless Pioneers Who Changed the World **RACHEL IGNOTOFSKY**	*Mira, Royal Detective*	*37 Words*
Brave Girl: Clara and the Shirtwaist Makers Strike **MICHELLE MARKEL**	*Food Network Star Kids*	*Under Pressure: The U.S. Women's World Cup Team*
Say Something **PETER REYNOLDS**	*Project Mc^2*	*Tiny Shoulders: Rethinking Barbie*
A Computer called Katherine **SUZANNE SLADE**	*Catie's Amazing Machines*	*Maya Angelou: And Still I Rise*
Strong is the New Pretty **KATE T. PARKER**		*Becoming*

Add your favorites here:

BOOKS	TV SERIES	DOCS FOR GROWN UPS

3 KEY BUILDING BLOCKS
for Embracing Ambition
1
2 3

Push Back on Perfection
Learn to Fail Forward!!
Prime Her for Power

PART 2
Ambition Reflection

Use this space to record notes and reflections,
as well as the ways you interacted with your girl.

Research shows that we can increase our propensity
to problem-solve through free drawing, and putting our
ideas into images on paper without rigid constraint.

Use this space to draw a reflection of the **Ambition**
chapters, and your interactions with your girl.

Our Game Plan

Use this space to write out your commitments to growing
your ambition together. Refer to the challenges and
exercises that inspired you most, and note how you will
turn to them – and each other – when you need
an ambition boost.

____

____

____

____

____

____

____

____

AMBITION RESOURCES

• • • •

 Organizations/Initiatives

- ***Lean In Girls*** is a leadership program that empowers girls to become self-assured, resilient and inclusive everyday leaders, and inspires them to lead boldly. At the heart of *Lean In Girls* is a leadership curriculum for girls and young teens who identify with the girlhood experience (ages 11 to 15). With a balance of strength-building activities and real talk on important topics, like bias and allyship, participants learn to embrace their leadership superpowers and reject limiting stereotypes about what girls can't do. **leaningirls.org**

- ***Girl Scouts of USA*** helps girls discover the fun, friendship and power of girls together. Girls grow courageous and strong through a wide variety of enriching experiences, such as field trips, skill-building sports clinics, community service projects, cultural exchanges, and environmental stewardships. *Girl Scouts* helps girls develop their full individual potential; relate to others with increasing understanding, skill, and respect; develop values to guide their actions and provide the foundation for sound decision-making; and contribute to the improvement of society through their abilities, leadership skills, and cooperation with others. *Girl Scouts* is a way of life that brings out the best in your girl, even in the most challenging of times. While they're learning about STEM, the outdoors, entrepreneurship and important life skills, *Girl Scouts* are also discovering new ways to make their family and community stronger, kinder and better for everyone. **girlscouts.org**

- ***Girls Who Code*** is a non-profit organization with a mission to close the gender gap in technology, and to transform the perception of how a programmer looks, and what they do. They offer a wide range of programs designed to support girls' and young womens' interest in the field of computer science. **girlswhocode.com**

AMBITION RESOURCES

● ● ● ●

▌ Books

- *Ambitious Girl* by Meena Harris
- *What Girls Need* by Marisa Porges, PhD
- *Girls Without Limits* by Dr. Lisa Hinkelman

▦ Articles

- "**Ambition: Femininity and Climbing the Ladder of Success**" by Audrey Nelson, PhD. *Psychology Today*, January 2022
- "**They Believe in Ambitious Women. But They Also See the Costs**" by Claire Cain Miller. *NY Times*, April 2021

♫ Podcast Episodes

- **ParentData with Emily Oster:** *High Achieving Kids*
- **Pursue What Matters with Dr. Melissa Smith** – Episode 100: *Embrace Ambition*

▶ Video Links

- **What if Women Built the World They Want to See?** *Girls Garage* Founder and Executive Director, Emily Pilloton-Lam, talks about putting power into the hands of young women and gender-expansive youth. In her talk, she dreams of inclusive construction sites and dares to ask: What if women built the world they want to see? In true Girls Garage fashion, Emily dazzled the audience with a live demo of her own woodworking skills...while giving the talk!
- **Jennifer Wallace – Never Enough: When Achievement Culture Becomes Toxic and What We Can Do About It.** Award-winning reporter, Jennifer Breheny Wallace, investigates the deep roots of toxic achievement culture, and finds ways to fight back. Through deep research and interviews with today's leading child psychologists, Wallace shows what kids need from the adults is not more pressure, but to feel like they matter, and have intrinsic self-worth not contingent upon external achievements.

KING
junior

Compassion

CHAPTER 9

Build Compassion

Embedding compassion rounds out our efforts to become a true advocate for the girls in our lives. The dictionary defines compassion as: *deep awareness of the suffering of another accompanied by the wish to relieve it.* Compassion means we care about others, treat them with kindness, and feel a strong desire to help people in need. It's easy to confuse compassion with empathy, so here is a simple breakdown.

What is compassion vs empathy?

While both involve responding to other people's emotions, they differ in focus. **Empathy** is characterized by an awareness of other people's emotional experiences, and an attempt to feel those same emotions from their perspective. **Compassion** is characterized by the desire to take action to help the other person. Compassion is *empathy in action.*

Having compassion also means that you:

1. Offer understanding and **kindness** to others when they fail or make mistakes, rather than judging them harshly.
2. Realize that suffering, failure and imperfection are part of the shared human experience, and create a **deeper connection to others**.
3. Experience benefits such as increased happiness through practicing **mindfulness**-focused behaviors on a regular basis.

Studies indicate that compassion is one of the traits people find most attractive in others. Decades of research has shown that compassion is the overarching trait that brings out the best in oneself, as well as others. According to neuroscientist, Dr. Jean Decety (2010), various studies have shown that children around four years of age can understand and show empathy for another person's perspective and their reactions to an event. Therefore, learning how to transform that empathy into action can encourage and embed compassion in our children. Research has also shown that practicing compassion not only makes the individual happier, but also creates an environment that elevates everyone around them. **Compassion is contagious...in a good way!**

Our goal is to encourage our girls to take action and show sympathy, understanding, concern, and support when they see others suffering, but (and this is crucial), our goal is also to **encourage girls to show that support towards themselves**. We want them to look inward for validation rather than seeking only the approval of others. We want girls to learn how to build resilience and confidence. This is what we refer to as **Self-Compassion**.

In 2007, I became a coach for the *Girls on the Run* program, which works with groups of girls in grades 3-5 to build confidence and other important life skills through dynamic, interactive lessons, and physical activity. I returned in 2023 to coach when my daughter joined a team in 4th grade. On a sunny day in April, I was preparing to coach an afternoon practice with a lesson focused on making healthy choices. I took two large poster boards and drew a large grid of boxes on each. Then I filled each box with a different healthy choice, such as being a good friend, encouraging others, showing gratitude, exercising regularly, eating well, and getting enough sleep. It's important to note that both posters contained identical healthy choices. The girls were asked to walk or run laps around the school playground and, after each lap, to mark their initials in one of the boxes on the poster boards. The first poster indicated healthy choices **they felt confident in making**; the second indicated healthy choices **they felt challenged to choose**.

As the girls marked their choices, I began to see a troubling trend. Once they had finished, I pulled them together in a half-circle and we studied the posters. Together, we celebrated the healthy choices they felt confident choosing. But then I paused. I looked each girl in the eye and shared what I had observed on the "challenging choice" poster. Every single girl had marked their initials in the same box: "be kind to myself". As I repeated it again slowly, the girls shuffled uncomfortably.

I told them, "You may not realize this, but all of us have moments when we don't say the kindest things to ourselves. Most of us battle with a bully in our brain who tells us we aren't smart enough, or pretty enough, or just *enough*". I expressed how important it is that we all learn to talk to ourselves with kindness, and that these thoughts can hurt us if we don't learn how to turn them around. But this skill is not as easy as it sounds.

For the next 20 minutes, we asked the girls to write down a negative thought or unkind thing they have said to themselves. They wrote things like: "I'm the worst at math"; "I hate my hair, it never looks like everyone else"; "I'm never going to be able to run a 5K. I am too slow". We divided the girls into pairs and asked them to take one lap around the school and work together to reframe the statements into something more positive. Why did we partner them up? The truth is that it's often easier to cheer somebody else on, and find the positive in others, than it is to do it for ourselves. Learning how to lean on each other, and vocalize out-loud a positive statement, has profound effects on our inner self-worth. I'll never forget hearing each of those girls share their newly-formed positive statement with me after their lap. You could feel the energy shift and the camaraderie strengthen after this important lesson.

Would you describe yourself as a compassionate person?

Can you think of a recent moment when you noticed someone suffering, and took action to support them? Or a time when you felt a strong bond with someone going through a hard time?

Compassion is both innate (meaning you naturally possess it), and can also be learned and enhanced. It's like a muscle that can be strengthened with relevant exercises – (or it can deteriorate and weaken). In other words, your capacity for compassion can expand if you choose to strengthen it.

Between the ages of 8 and 12, girls experience a marked increase in self-aware-ness, self-reflection, and their ability to understand something from a different perspective. These skills contribute to the development of a sense of identity and self-concept (Butler, 1998). This stage is crucial for our girls, and it gives us an opportunity to role-model the behaviors we want them to learn. Take this as an example: a neighbor is going through a tough time, so we show our concern and state, *"That sounds very hard, and I'm worried about how they can care for themselves. Let's offer to pick up some groceries or drop a meal off for them."* We want to focus on teaching compassion in real-time, as well as theoretically.

It is important to focus on all emotional situations – not just sad ones – when we are teaching self-compassion. So, let's also create moments where we share our excitement, and explain why we are excited. *"I just found out my good friend is starting a new business. I'm so happy and excited to support her!"*

Over the next three chapters, we will delve into a series of **Challenges** that provide step-by-step guidance to support conversations with your girl. The chal-lenges will benefit both your girl and you, as her fierce advocate. Consider each chapter as a building block in the foundation of embedding compassion within her.

CHAPTER 10

Supercharge Her Self-Kindness

"If you want others to be happy, practice compassion.
If you want to be happy, practice compassion."
— Dalai Lama, The Art of Happiness

Self-compassion means that, when we are having a difficult time, make mistakes, or notice something we don't like about ourselves, we act in the same way towards ourselves *as we would towards others*. Tuning in to those feelings of discomfort allows us to push back on that bully in our brain. Instead of just ignoring our pain with a "stiff upper lip" mentality, we tell ourselves, "Hey, this is a really difficult time right now," and ask ourselves the question, "What do we need in this moment?"

In a noisy world, where girls feel the negative effects of constant comparison to others, learning to comfort, care for, and soothe themselves is more important than ever. Let's teach our girls to show kindness to themselves instead of spiraling into a harsh inner dialogue.

Self-compassionate people recognize that being imperfect, failing and experiencing life's difficulties are inevitable. They are gentle with themselves when confronted with painful experiences, rather than getting angry when life falls short of their expectations. We can't always be – or get – what we want and, when this reality is denied or fought against, suffering increases in the form of stress, frustration and self-criticism. When we accept our reality with sympathy and kindness, we experience greater emotional self-control.

With that in mind, let's dive into the next set of challenges, which will strengthen your girl's self-compassion through inner kindness.

Girls and women often sabotage themselves with negative self-talk, which can sound like, *"I can't..."*, or *"I'm bad at..."*, or *"I'm the worst..."*. We must teach our girls how to reframe their thoughts by countering it with self-talk that is both positive and realistic.

For example, instead of saying:

"I'm terrible at math."

reframe the challenge as:

"I'm working really hard to understand my math homework."

That's more realistic and valuable than having them say, *"I will get 100 percent on my next math quiz,"* because it focuses on their effort, not the outcome. The following exercise is a powerful strategy that I use weekly with women of all ages. Girls *and* women deserve to feel worthy without changing themselves, or letting the bully in their brain get the best of them.

When our girls are tempted to be harsh, critical, and judgmental with themselves, let's encourage them to choose compassion. Help them to acknowledge their own suffering, and note how it makes them feel human, and that they are not alone.

Write down a negative thought the bully in your
brain says, and reframe the negative thought with
a positive statement.

INSTEAD OF   ⟶   **SAY**

"I am the worst at math."   ⟶   *"I'm trying my best to learn new math skills and eventually I will figure it out."*

"I hate my hair. It never looks like everyone else's."   ⟶   *"I have my grandmother's hair and that makes me proud."*

⟶

⟶

⟶

⟶

⟶

CHALLENGE

Kind-Writing

In this exercise, you and your girl will practice writing kind, encouraging and comforting statements.

Use one page for you, and one for her. Let her doodle on scrap paper while you write first, which allows you to role-model self-compassion. Then let her read your words before she takes her turn. Focus on using kind, understanding words of comfort. Maybe you recently went through a hard time, made a mistake, or experienced frustration with how you behaved in a situation.

Examples are:

"It's okay. You messed up, but it wasn't the end of the world. I understand how frustrated you were, and you just lost it. Maybe you can try being extra patient with your friends this week, so they know you were having a hard time last week."

"I know you really want to achieve that goal, but change is never simple. It's easier if you stop being hard on yourself. My mistakes show that I'm growing and learning. It's okay to make mistakes and forgive myself."

Name: ____

Name: ___________________________________

Kind-Writing

When you take the lead in role-modeling self-kindness, and demonstrate the language you can use to soothe and support yourself, you give your girl permission to do the same. She may have questions about your statements so help her understand why you have written what you have. And give her plenty of time – and even physical space – to write her own letter.

NOTES

CHALLENGE
"What Happened?"

A great way to teach your girl self-kindness is to show her a scenario, and then ask her, **"What happened?"** and **"How do you feel?"**

For example, let's consider a picture of a child crying because she fell down while ice skating, or because her ice cream fell on the floor. Ask your girl:

"What happened?"
Encourage her to describe the scene. Discuss the situation and explore if this ever happened to her or someone she knows.

"How do you feel?"
This question works on two levels. The first encourages her to explore how she would feel if the same thing happened to her; the second explores her compassion toward the person in the scene. Depending on your girl's age, it's possible to help her see why another person would feel a certain way by looking for "clues" in the scene. The more realistic the scenario, the better. Ask her what she sees in the picture that makes her feel that way, and then ask her to point those clues out.

"What Happened?"

According to bestselling author and vulnerability expert, Brené Brown, when we acknowledge personal vulnerabilities and mistakes that can bring about shame, we can practice letting go of who we're "supposed to be" and embrace "who we really are". We can be brave enough to accept being imperfect! Practicing self-kindness addresses the judgment and secrecy of shame. We are not alone in how we feel. Rather than talking to ourselves harshly, let's teach our girls to treat themselves with care, understanding, and support when they are experiencing shame. Through self-compassion, they will learn to embrace these vulnerabilities, and not allow themselves to feel negatively affected.

NOTES

____

____

____

____

CHAPTER 11

Deepen Her Connection to Others

Common humanity is the understanding that unpleasant feelings are part of the human experience and that suffering is universal. This might sound like a bummer but it's the absolute truth – and it can be incredibly freeing! We are connected not only by our joys, but also our struggles, heartaches, shame and fears. Common humanity is a key component in what connects us. Being human means being imperfect. Shame is an inherently human trait that can encourage a connection with others instead of letting ourselves feel isolated and alone. Why else would we say *"you are only human"* to comfort someone who has made a mistake? When we're in touch with our common humanity, we remember that feelings of inadequacy and disappointment are universally experienced.

Eight-year-old Maria has beautiful brown eyes and an infectious giggle. Her favorite animal is a dog, and her favorite color is purple. Maria loves to bake cookies with her Abuela after school, and she has many friends in her 3rd grade class. But Maria wasn't always this happy. When she moved to the US two years ago, she didn't know anyone in her class, nor speak any English. She played alone at recess, and sat by herself at lunch. She felt lonely and worried that she would never belong.

Then, one Monday morning, Maria's teacher introduced a new student to their class. Jia Li had just moved to the US from China with her family. Jia Li took the seat next to Maria and sat quietly through the math lesson, without looking or speaking to anyone. Maria noticed that Jia Li kept to herself at recess and sat alone at lunch. "Wow, she is not being very friendly!" Maria thought to herself.

That afternoon she told her Abuela about the new student in her class, and commented on the fact that she didn't talk or play with anyone during recess. Abuela reminded Maria that it was hard for her, too, when she had first moved to the US and didn't know anyone.

The following morning, when Jia Li arrived at class, Maria remembered her Abuela's words. She noticed Jia Li's purple shirt with a picture of a puppy on it. Smiling kindly, Maria said, "I like your shirt – purple is my favorite color!" Jia Li smiled shyly. At recess, Maria found Jia Li sitting alone and invited her to jump rope together. They soon discovered that they were both working on learning to double jump with the rope. At lunch, Maria introduced Jia Li to another friend in their class, and they all bonded over a shared love of PB&J sandwiches!

By the end of the day, Maria and Jia Li had discovered lots in common, and Jia Li left the classroom with a smile on her face.

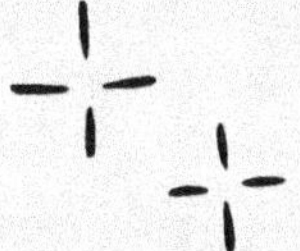

CHALLENGE

We Are Only Human!

In this exercise, we will embrace our emotions and experiment with our connection to the larger human experience. With your girl, use this space to write down some examples of when you felt a greater connection to others, or shared an experience.

Examples:

Let's say you shared this story:

> *"Last week I was super frustrated when I was late for an important doctor's appointment across town. There was a lot of traffic, and I was angry at myself for not leaving earlier."*

Next, practice out loud how you would relate this experience to being "only human". You could say:

> *"Everyone overreacts sometimes and it's common to underestimate travel time...it's only human."*

Next, ask your girl to share something that frustrated or excited her, and how she could relate that experience to being "only human."

We Are Only Human!

We Are Only Human!

Pay attention to your girl's use of words to express her emotions. For example, *frustration* is not having things exactly as you want, but it is often accompanied by an irrational, but pervasive, sense of isolation. Oftentimes, when we are experiencing a challenging emotion, we feel like we are the only person suffering, or the only person that makes mistakes. Remind your girl that all humans suffer and make mistakes. Self-compassion means recognizing that suffering and failure are part of the shared human experience. We all go through it. We are not alone.

It is helpful to build your girl's emotional vocabulary by introducing more complex, nuanced emotions such as loneliness, grief, jealousy, anticipation, wonder, gratitude, hope and peace.

Teaching your girl the definitions of key emotions will broaden her vocabulary and make it easier to express herself. When you hear or see her experiencing one of these emotions, share your observation: *"It's been two weeks since your friend moved away. Are you feeling lonely?"* Model using specific words to describe your own emotions so she understands that everyone has feelings: *"When I take a walk outside, it helps me feel peaceful"*; or *"I felt really nervous today when I couldn't find my keys to leave on time for work."*

We Are Only Human!

Let's build your girl's emotional vocabulary by introducing more complex, nuanced emotions.

Lonely: *being alone when you don't want to be or feeling alone when you are with others*	**Energized:** *have enthusiasm and determination to do something*	**Disappointed:** *discouraged or sad because what you hoped for didn't happen*
Satisfied: *happy with what you have or the way things are; content*	**Passionate:** *very strong feelings or belief about something*	**Jealous:** *wanting something that other people have*
Grateful: *feeling or expressing thanks for good things in your life*	**Thrilled:** *extremely happy or excited about something*	**Proud:** *really happy with something great that you or someone else did*
Puzzled: *unable to understand and feeling confused*	**Wondering:** *desire to know or learn something*	**Grieving:** *emotional reaction to the loss of someone or something important to you*
Nervous: *scared or worried about something that is happening or might happen*	**Concerned:** *worried about someone or something because it is important to you or affects you*	**Frustrating:** *tense, unhappy feeling when you can't do something you should be able to do or want to do*
Hopeful: *feeling or inspiring optimism about a future event*	**Worried:** *to think about problems or fears; feeling anxious or upset*	**Adore:** *to love and respect someone or something very much*
Uncertain: *unsure or undecided*	**Amazed:** *surprised and overjoyed*	**Peaceful:** *quiet, calm, free from disturbance*

Encourage Kind Impulses

Use descriptive praise when you see your child reaching out to someone else with compassion. This reinforces their impulse to act with compassion, and fosters greater human connection. This might sound like:

"Thank you for giving me a hug when I was feeling frustrated yesterday. That was just what I needed to help me feel better."

"That was a thoughtful note you wrote to your friend. I know she's sad about moving away, and your note will remind her of how much you care about her."

For a six or seven-year-old girl, compassion might look like giving a hug, making a card, or saying something kind to a friend or family member who is feeling sad. It can also look like reaching out to a peer who has been left out of a play date, or hearing about a community need and wanting to do something to help.

Encourage Kind Impulses

When an eight to ten-year-old-girl sees or hears others suffering, she may want to know "why?". This could show up as seeking information through conversations with you, or reading, experimenting, observing, and asking questions. Eight-year-olds enjoy having the opportunity to solve problems independently. Let your girl show you how much she can do!

You don't have to have all the answers. Instead, encourage her to think about what actions she could take to support others in need. Offering our girls this type of guidance and support helps them develop the habits they need to cultivate a kind culture around themselves at school, in their communities, and beyond.

NOTES

____

____

____

____

CHAPTER 12

Master Mindfulness

Mindfulness is one of the fastest-growing health trends in the $4.5 trillion wellness industry, with nearly 14% of people having tried meditation in the United States. As a result, the centuries-old practice of meditation has gone mainstream, even reaching our children through global school initiatives to help kids learn skills to navigate stress. New research on mindfulness and meditation has proven there are benefits for people who practice for as little as ten minutes a day! From controlling and managing pain, to lowering blood pressure and lessening the symptoms of depression, the results are tangible and worth exploring for our girls.

Today's teenagers report an alarming increase in rates of anxiety and depression. One study found that the number of girls who often felt nervous, worried or fearful jumped by 55 percent over a five-year period. Lisa Damour, psychotherapist and bestselling author of *Untangled* and *Under Pressure*, has closely monitored the rising levels of tension in girls, and confirms they are more likely than boys to struggle with psychological stress and tension. Research shows that a staggering 31% of girls and young women experience symptoms of anxiety, compared with 13% of boys and young men. Mindfulness is a worthwhile remedy to help us and our girls combat these difficult trends.

mindfulness noun

mind·ful·ness

an intentional state of focused, nonjudgmental awareness that can allow you to observe thoughts and feelings
as they are, without trying to suppress or deny them

Teaching your girl how to master mindfulness will bring awareness to the strategies she can use to navigate stress and ease the painful emotions caused by harsh
self-judgment. Being mindful means having your mind focus on what you are
doing in the present. It's the opposite of rushing, or doing too many things at
once (despite the temptation in the modern world to multi-task). You focus on
what you're doing in a calm state and stay present with your focus. We cannot
ignore our pain and feel compassion for it at the same time. Therefore, practicing
mindfulness offers us – and our girls – a greater capacity for compassion.

Our goal is to help our girls take a balanced approach to their negative emotions
so that their feelings are neither suppressed nor exaggerated. Helping her practice mindfulness, allows her to put her own situation into a larger perspective
without minimizing her pain. Bringing mindful awareness to negative emotions
and thoughts allows us to observe and determine a response – not just a reaction.
Have you ever had one of those moments where you were triggered, and reacted
in a way that did not make you feel any better? The strategies in this chapter will
help girls choose healthier responses to better protect their wellbeing. Think of it
like this: you are helping your girl to create a "classroom" in her mind and heart,
so she can learn more about herself and experiment with healthy ways to navigate
her experiences.

Start with Mindful Breathing

Kids, just like grown ups, have a lot on their minds. They can find it challenging to track what they have to do, from homework to playdates. A great place to start is with mindful breathing. Find a quiet place with your girl, and explain that this exercise is a simple and easy way to learn how to focus on the present.

Step 1

The goal is to pause and take a few slow and easy breaths. Explain that, for a few minutes, you will focus on breathing – instead of letting your minds wander. It's worth learning how to be mindful at a time when you're not in a rush, so you are better prepared when you are.

Step 2

For the first two-three breaths, read these directions to your girl:

"Notice your breathing. Breathe in through your nose. Breathe out through your nose. Try to let your breathing be slow and easy. Breathe in. Breathe out. Notice how your body feels as you breathe."

Start with Mindful Breathing

"Can you feel the air tickle your nose as you breathe? Does the air feel warm or cool? Can you feel your belly, your chest, or your rib cage move in and out as you breathe? If you want, you can put one hand on your belly or your chest. Let each breath bring you calmness. If you want, when you breathe out, you can sigh out some stress (show her how to do this by making a sound like 'haaa' or 'hmmm'). If your mind wanders, and you start thinking of other things, gently guide your mind back to your breathing. See if you can take four slow, calming breaths."

Allow her to continue for one-two minutes in silence without guiding her.

Step 3

When you are finished, encourage your girl to slowly open her eyes. Ask her to notice how she feels.

Start with Mindful Breathing

Step 4

Discuss times when mindful breathing could help each of you. For example, you could try mindful breathing:

- *in the morning, to get your day off to a great start before you jump out of bed*

- *at bedtime to help you get a peaceful night's sleep*

- *when taking a big test at school, to train your attention and focus better*

- *when you're dealing with a big emotion – like frustration, anger, or anxiety – as a way to calm you down.*

According to a study by Duke University, more than 40% of our daily activities are done out of habit. That means almost half of our day is on autopilot. Imagine if you can help your girl (and yourself!) use mindful breathing as a positive daily ritual. With more practice, she could tap into this valuable skill at a moment's notice to find peace and quiet whenever she needs it.

Start with Mindful Breathing

Use this space to reflect on how you felt after the mindful breathing technique, and when you could use it in the future.

____

____

____

____

____

____

____

____

____

Children as young as two years of age can benefit from meditation and the peace of mind it brings.

At its core, meditation is a practice of mindfulness and self-awareness. Meditation can teach kids how to observe stressful thoughts without judgment, and learn to relax when they need it most. Imagine a bowling alley lane where the bumpers are raised on each side to support your ability to fire the ball toward the pins. The bumpers are not meant to stop the ball, but to guide it forward. The ball is your thoughts, and the meditation practice is the bumpers used to gently guide your focus. Not to change them, but to help you stay in the awareness lane. Meditation can heighten optimism and positive feelings, increase stress immunity, enhance feelings of closeness, connectedness, and social bonding, and decrease post-traumatic stress symptoms.

Meditation for Kids

There is resounding evidence of the benefits of teaching kids how to meditate such as:

- *Improved sleep*

- *Increased focus and prolonged attention span*

- *Reduced stress and anxiety*

- *Stronger mental resilience*

- *Improved emotional regulation*

- *Improved working memory capacity*

- *Increased self-awareness and empathy*

Take a Mindfulness Field Trip

There are so many opportunities to actively observe the world around you in our daily life. Let's take a trip to the supermarket as an example. When you are standing in line to check out, don't get distracted by your phone, or stress about how fast the other line is moving (I'm guilty of both!). Instead, take a moment to consider the common humanity of the people who made your grocery trip possible – the people who grew and transported the food, stocked the shelves, or the cashier and grocery bagger who are about to help you. Take a moment of appreciation for each of them. Take your time explaining this to younger girls under age 9 who may have a lot of questions about each person's job at the supermarket. This exercise is a way of demonstrating how we can cultivate compassion and be mindful in our everyday experiences.

Take a Mindfulness Field Trip

FINAL CHALLENGE
Meditate with Affirmations

In different chapters of this workbook, we have offered affirmation statements as an opportunity to teach your girl how to speak encouragingly to herself, and redirect her thoughts to a positive place. Teach her how to use affirmations with intention. Encourage her to breathe gently, and recite the phrases silently or out loud.

Take turns repeating these phrases and adjust the words in any way you wish. Sometimes the use of affirmations can feel awkward or frustrating, so it is especially important to encourage your girl to be patient and kind toward herself. Teach her to use these affirmative statements toward herself and, when she feels strong enough, encourage her to direct these kind thoughts towards someone she cares about.

I trust myself.

I can learn from
my mistakes,
but I am not a mistake.

I can learn and grow.

My emotions are mine.
They are not bad or good.
They are helpful or
unhelpful in a situation.

I deserve
to take breaks.

My future
is positive.

Mistakes
are necessary.

I am aware
of this moment.

I am trustworthy.

I have
good intentions.

I can make healthy
decisions and choices.

I am worthy and
valuable, regardless
of my achievements.

Progress is more
important than
perfection.

I can learn and grow
from my challenges.

I am filled with
loving kindness.

I deserve
to be happy.

3 KEY BUILDING BLOCKS
to Build Compassion
1
2 3

Supercharge Her Self-Kindness

Deepen Her Connection to Others

Master Mindfulness

PART 3

Compassion Reflection

Use this space to record notes and reflections, as well as the ways you interacted with your girl.

Research shows that we can increase our propensity to problem-solve through free drawing, and putting our ideas into images on paper without rigid constraint.

Use this space to draw a reflection of the **Compassion** chapters, and your interactions with your girl.

Our Game Plan

Use this space to write out your commitments to growing your compassion together. Refer to the challenges and exercises that inspired you most, and note how you will turn to them – and each other – when you need a compassion boost.

COMPASSION RESOURCES

● ● ● ●

♥ Organizations/Initiatives

- *Girls On The Run* is a network of local councils offering programming at schools and community sites across the United States and Canada. Their mission is to inspire girls to be joyful, healthy and confident, using a fun, experience-based curriculum, which creatively integrates running. They provide evidence-based programs that inspire girl empowerment by building confidence, kindness and decision making skills. **girlsontherun.org**
- *Fearlessly Girl* is working to create a world in which young women are kinder to themselves and each other, feel confident to express themselves authentically, and are empowered to fearlessly take the lead in their lives, schools & communities. Their Fearlessly Kind school programming is an engaging, immersive, and interactive school-wide educational program, thoughtfully curated with the help of educators, counselors and youth workers for young women in 5th to 8th grade. **fearlesslygirl.com**

▌ Books

- *Raising Girls Who Like Themselves* by Kasey Edwards
- *Raising Good Humans* by Hunter Clarke-Fields
- *The Power of One* by Trudy Ludwig

▦ Articles

- "Why Women Need Fierce Self-Compassion" by Dr. Kristin Neff. *self-compassion.org*, March 2019
- "The Promise of Self-Compassion for Stressed Out Teens" by Rachel Simmons. *NY Times*, February 2018

● ● ● ●

♫ Podcast Episodes

- **:10 for Tweens and Teens Podcast with Stephanie Valdez** – Episode 4: *Be the Good*
- **Good Inside with Dr. Becky Kennedy:** *How to Not Raise an @$$h0le*

▶ Video Links

- **Educating the Whole Child (and Adult) with Emotional Literacy by Mark Brackett.** TEDxGoldenGateEd. Dr. Marc Brackett introduces the Mood Meter, which offers strategies to teach children how to manage their emotional lives.
- **Social Justice Parenting by Dr. Traci Baxley.** TEDxBrowardCollege. Dr. Traci Baxley discusses new ideas in parenting that can lead to more curiosity for learning, and turn fear into motivation for positive change.

Congratulations on reaching the end of the book!

I'm so thrilled you made the effort to learn, grow, reflect, and connect with your girl! Whether you completed the whole workbook, or only managed a single challenge, you took the time to show her you care, and that she deserves to take care of herself. Remember, this is an imperfect journey. I'm sure, like me, you experienced moments that were better or worse than you anticipated. Some topics may have felt familiar; others more challenging. But, know that you can return to the *Girls &* workbook any time you need support.

My early childhood experiences ingrained in me that we all deserve to pursue our potential, cultivate our confidence and embrace our ambition. We each have a vision for what success and happiness look and feel like. I've learned that defining success and wellness on my own terms makes a difference. It enables me to prioritize my happiness, and give myself permission to feel the range of emotions that accompany those periods of growth and times when I needed to slow down.

Over the years, I've witnessed so many women caught between what they truly want from life, and the unexpected and jarring ways the world judges their every move. Too often girls and women feel invisible, unprepared and overwhelmed; unworthy of advocating for their needs, or expressing their opinions.

Girls & is determined to change that. I want my girls, your girls – *all of us* – to bypass the toxic confidence roller coaster. We have infinite strength and power within us. Let's learn to walk proudly towards whatever it is we want (and deserve).

Please remember: you are not alone. Your girl is not alone. The more we strive to remind each other that it is possible to lead change for ourselves – and those around us – the greater the impact on women everywhere. Every effort you've made to connect with your girl fuels this movement. Every conversation matters. So, let's continue empowering your girl to become her own best advocate.

One final thing. Your stories, breakthroughs, feedback and ideas are extremely impactful. If you feel inspired to share your experience with the *Girls &* workbook, please contact us here:

www.GirlsWorkbook.com
JoanKuhl.com/GirlsWorkbook
GirlsWorkbook@gmail.com
@GirlsWorkbook

ABOUT THE AUTHOR

Joan Kuhl is a passionate champion for inclusive and equitable leadership, working to change how women rise and thrive at work and in their personal lives. She is an author, sought-after speaker, thought leader, conference & workshop designer, consultant, MBA advisor, executive coach, and research project leader with decades of global research and consulting experience. Over 850+ employees in 30 countries have participated in her signature virtual training, Stay To Lead, a leadership retention and advancement program. Joan has worked with corporate leadership development teams to track the positive impact of her global leadership training programs on women's retention, engagement, and promotions.

Joan has a long history of involvement in organizations that serve girls (Girls Inc of NYC, Girl Scouts, Girls Hope of Pittsburgh, Step Up For Women, US Soccer SheBelieves, Girls On The Run, Girls Leadership and LiveGirl) serving as a board member, content designer, coach and volunteer.

She is the author of *Dig Your Heels In: Navigate Corporate BS and Build the Company You Deserve* (April 2019) and *Misunderstood Millennial Talent* (2016). Her expertise has been featured in the *New York Times, Harvard Business Review,* CNBC, *SUCCESS,* and *The Washington Post.* Joan is a Contributor to ForbesWomen, and NBC Know Your Value.

Joan earned her B.S.B.A. at the University of Pittsburgh and her M.B.A. at Rutgers University, where she studied global management in Shanghai and Beijing, China. Joan enjoys watching women's sports and cheering for the US Women's National Soccer Team with her husband and two daughters.

Girls &

Copyright © 2024 by Joan Kuhl.

All rights reserved. No part of this book may be reproduced in any form or by any electronic or mechanical means, including information storage and retrieval systems, without written permission from the author, except for the use of brief quotations in a book review.

First Edition

ISBN 9781662951251 (paperback)
ISBN 9781662951268 (ebook)

Design by Liliana Guia
Illustrations by Polina Tomtosova/iStockphoto
Photography by kool99/iStockphoto (10); Kate T. Parker (27, 55, 92); andresr/iStockphoto (52); Kerkez/iStockphoto (71); FatCamera/iStockphoto (97); Karen Morneau Photography (142)